PARTY FINGER FOOD TUTORIAL

50 EXCITING RECIPES UNDER 30 MINUTES

J.LUIZ

Disclaimer

The information contained i is meant to serve as a comprehensive collection of strategies that the author of this eBook has done research about. Summaries, strategies, tips and tricks are only recommendation by the author, and reading this eBook will not guarantee that one's results will exactly mirror the author's results. The author of the eBook has made all reasonable effort to provide current and accurate information for the readers of the eBook. The author and it's associates will not be held liable for any unintentional error or omissions that may be found. The material in the eBook may include information by third parties. Third party materials comprise of opinions expressed by their owners. As such, the author of the eBook does not assume responsibility or liability for any third party material or opinions. Whether because of the progression of the internet, or the unforeseen changes in company policy and editorial submission guidelines, what is

TABLE OF CONTENTS

INTRODUCTION

Who doesn't love party finger food? They are not only delicious; they are essential to making sure you are getting your guests smiling.

What Are Finger Foods?

Finger foods are ideally small, bite-sized foods that are meant to be eaten directly with your hands, no utensils required! Instead of fork and knives, people will often serve these mini appetizers with skewers or toothpicks for easy eating!

If it takes you more than three bites to finish it, it is most likely not a true finger food! One bite foods are the best kind of appetizers to serve because they require no napkins and little to no mess!

Finger foods have been around for some time now. Believe it or not, they became popular around the prohibition era when they had speakeasy bars. Cocktails would be served illegally and they would accompany those illegal drinks with small foods that were easy to serve and eat to keep people happy and also keep them drinking!

Fancy fingers foods are perfect for cocktail parties and special events or holidays like Weddings or New Year's Eve! They are sure to impress and perfect for adults!

Let's get started then!

MINI-BITES

1. Burrito bites

Ingredient

- 1 can Diced Tomatoes

- 1 cup Instant rice

- ⅓ cup Water

- 1 Green pepper, diced

- 2 Green onions, sliced

- 2 cups Shredded cheddar cheese, divided

- 1 can Ranch Style Refried Beans (16 oz)

- 10 Flour tortillas (6-7")

- 1 cup Salsa

a) Preheat oven to 350'F. Spray a 9x12" baking dish with PAM; set aside.

b) In a medium saucepan, combine RO*TEL, rice and water; heat to a boil.

c) Reduce heat, cover and simmer 1 minute. Remove from heat and let sit 5 minutes or until all liquid is absorbed. Stir in pepper, onions and 1 cup cheese.

d) Spread about 3 tablespoons beans over each tortilla to within $\frac{1}{8}$" from edge. Layer rice mixture over beans; roll up. Place seam side down in prepared baking dish; cover with foil.

e) Bake in preheated oven 25 minutes or until hot. Cut tortillas into 4 pieces and place on platter. Top with salsa and cheese. Top with salsa and cheese. Return to oven and bake 5 minutes or until cheese melts.

2. Chicken nut bites

Ingredient

- 1 cup Chicken broth

- ½ cup Butter

- 1 cup Flour

- 1 tablespoon Parsley

- 2 teaspoons Seasoned salt

- 2 teaspoons Worcestershire Sauce

- 34 teaspoons Celery seed

- $\frac{1}{2}$ teaspoon Paprika

- $\frac{1}{8}$ teaspoon Cayenne

- 4 large Eggs

- 2 Chicken breasts, poached, skinned

- $\frac{1}{4}$ cup Toasted almonds

a) Preheat oven to 400 degrees. In a heavy pan, combine broth and butter, and bring to a boil. Whisk in flour and seasoning.

b) Cook, whisking rapidly, until mixture leaves sides of pan and forms a smooth, compact ball. Remove from heat. Add eggs one at a time, beating well until mixture is shiny. Stir in chicken and almonds.

c) Drop by rounded teaspoonfuls onto greased baking sheets. Bake for 15 minutes. Freeze after baking.

3. Buffalo chicken fingers

- 2 cups almond flour

- 1 teaspoon salt

- 1 teaspoon black pepper

- 1 teaspoon dried parsley

- 2 large eggs

- 2 tablespoons full-fat canned coconut milk

- 2 pounds chicken tenders

- $1^1/_2$ cups Frank's RedHot Buffalo sauce

1 Preheat oven to 350°F.

2 Combine almond flour, salt, pepper, and parsley in a medium bowl and set aside.

3 Beat eggs and coconut milk together in a separate medium bowl.

4 Dip each chicken tender into egg mixture and then coat completely with almond flour mixture. Arrange coated tenders in a single layer on a baking sheet.

5 Bake 30 minutes, flipping once during cooking. Remove from oven and allow to cool 5 minutes.

6 Place chicken tenders in a large bowl and add buffalo sauce. Toss to coat completely.

4. Meatloaf muffins

- 1 pound ground beef

- 1 cup chopped spinach

- 1 large egg, lightly beaten

- $^1/_2$ cup shredded mozzarella cheese

- $^1/_4$ cup grated Parmesan cheese

- $^1/_4$ cup chopped yellow onion

- 2 tablespoons seeded and minced jalapeño pepper

1 Preheat oven to 350°F. Lightly grease each well of a muffin tin.

2 Combine all ingredients in large bowl and use your hands to mix.

3 Scoop an equal portion of meat mixture into each muffin tin and press down lightly. Bake 45 minutes or until internal temperature reaches 165°F.

5. Bacon avocado bites

- 2 large avocados, peeled and pitted

- 8 slices no-sugar-added bacon

- $1/2$ teaspoon garlic salt

1 Preheat oven to 425°F. Line a cookie sheet with parchment paper.

2 Cut each avocado into 8 equal-sized slices, making 16 slices total.

3 Cut each piece of bacon in half. Wrap a half slice of bacon around each piece of avocado. Sprinkle with garlic salt.

4 Place avocado on cookie sheet and bake 15 minutes. Turn oven to broil and continue to cook another 2–3 minutes until bacon becomes crispy.

6. Pizza bites

- 24 slices sugar-free pepperoni

- $^1/_2$ cup marinara sauce

- $^1/_2$ cup shredded mozzarella cheese

1 Turn on oven broiler.

2 Line a baking sheet with parchment paper and lay out pepperoni slices in a single layer.

3 Put 1 teaspoon marinara sauce on each pepperoni slice and spread out with a spoon. Add 1 teaspoon mozzarella cheese on top of marinara.

4 Put baking sheet in the oven and broil 3 minutes or until cheese is melted and slightly brown.

5 Remove from baking sheet and transfer to a paper towel-lined baking sheet to absorb excess grease.

7. Bacon and scallion bites

- $^1/_3$ cup almond meal

- 1 tablespoon unsalted butter, melted

- 1 (8-ounce) package cream cheese, softened to room temperature

- 1 tablespoon bacon grease

- 1 large egg

- 4 slices no-sugar-added bacon, cooked, cooled, and crumbled into bits

- 1 large green onion, tops only, thinly sliced

- 1 clove garlic, minced

- $^1/_8$ teaspoon black pepper

1 Preheat oven to 325°F.

2 In a small mixing bowl, combine almond meal and butter.

3 Line 6 cups of a standard-sized muffin tin with cupcake liners. Equally divide almond meal mixture among cups and press into the bottom gently with the back of a teaspoon. Bake in oven 10 minutes, then remove.

4 While the crust is baking, thoroughly combine cream cheese and bacon grease in a medium mixing bowl with a hand mixer. Add egg and blend until combined.

5 Fold bacon, onion, garlic, and pepper into cream cheese mixture with a spatula.

6 Divide mixture among cups, return to oven, and bake another 30-35 minutes until cheese sets. Edges may be slightly browned. To test doneness, insert toothpick into center. If it comes out clean, cheesecake is done.

7 Let cool 5 minutes and serve.

8. Bacon-wrapped chicken bites

- $3/4$ pound boneless, skinless chicken breast, cut into 1" cubes

- $1/2$ teaspoon salt

- $1/2$ teaspoon black pepper

- 5 slices no-sugar-added bacon

1 Preheat oven to 375°F.

2 Toss chicken with salt and pepper.

3 Cut each slice of bacon into 3 pieces and wrap each piece of chicken in a piece of bacon. Secure with a toothpick.

4 Put wrapped chicken on a broiler rack and bake 30 minutes, turning over halfway through cooking. Turn oven to broil and broil 3-4 minutes or until bacon is crispy.

9. Bacon-oyster bites

Ingredient
- 8 slices Bacon
- ½ cup Herbed seasoned stuffing
- 1 can (5-oz) oysters; chopped
- ¼ cup Water

a) Preheat oven to 350ø. Cut bacon slices in half and cook slightly. DO NOT OVERCOOK.
b) Bacon must be soft enough to roll easiiy around balls. Combine stuffing, oysters and water.
c) Roll into bite-sized balls, approximately 16.

d) Wrap balls in bacon. Bake at 350ø for 25 minutes. Serve warm.

10. Buffalo cauliflower bites

- 1 cup almond meal

- 1 teaspoon granulated garlic

- $1/2$ teaspoon dried parsley

- $1/2$ teaspoon salt

- 1 large egg

- 1 large head cauliflower, cut into bite-sized florets

- $1/2$ cup Frank's RedHot sauce

- $1/4$ cup ghee

1 Preheat oven to 400°F. Line a baking sheet with parchment paper.

2 Combine almond meal, garlic, parsley, and salt in a large sealable plastic bag and shake to mix.

3 Whisk egg in a large bowl. Add cauliflower and toss to coat completely.

4 Transfer cauliflower to bag filled with almond meal mixture and toss to coat.

5 Arrange cauliflower in a single layer on baking sheet and bake 30 minutes or until softened and slightly browned.

6 While cauliflower is baking, combine hot sauce and ghee in a small saucepan over low heat.

7 When cauliflower is cooked, combine cauliflower with hot sauce mixture in a large mixing bowl and toss to coat.

11. Chocolate Chili Mini Churros

Ingredients

Churros:

- 1 cup water
- 1/2 cup coconut oil or vegan butter
- 1 cup flour
- 1/4 tsp salt
- 3 eggs beaten
- Cinnamon Sugar Mixture
- 1/2 cup sugar1 tablespoon cinnamon

Directions:

a) Pre-heat oven to 400Combine water, coconut oil/butter and salt in a pot and bring to a boil.

b) Whisk in flour, stirring quickly until mixture turns into a ball.

c) Slowly stir in the eggs a little at a time, mixing continuously to make sure the eggs don't scramble.

d) Allow batter to cool slightly, and then transfer to your piping bag.

e) Pipe 3 inch long churros into rows on your greased baking sheet.

f) Bake in the oven for 10 minutes at 400 degrees and then broil on high for 1-2 minutes until your churros are golden brown.

g) Meanwhile, mix together cinnamon and sugar in a small dish.

h) Once churros are out of the oven, roll them into the cinnamon and sugar mix until fully coated. Set aside.

12. Bouillabaisse bites

Ingredient

- 24 mediums   Shrimp -- peeled and
- Deveined
- 24 mediums   Sea scallops
- 2 cups   Tomato sauce
- 1 can   Minced clams (6-1/2 oz)
- 1 tablespoon   Pernod

- 20Milliliters
- 1 Bay leaf
- 1 teaspoon   Basil
- $\frac{1}{2}$ teaspoon   Salt*
- $\frac{1}{2}$ teaspoon   Freshly ground pepper
- Garlic -- minced
- Saffron

a) Skewer shrimp and scallops on 8-inch bamboo skewers, using 1 shrimp and 1 scallop per skewer; wrap tail of shrimp around scallop.

b) Mix tomato sauce, clams, Pernod, garlic, bay leaf, basil, salt, pepper and saffron together in saucepan. Bring mixture to ge Arrange skewered fish in shallow baking dish.

c) Drizzle sauce over skewers. Bake, uncovered, at 350 degress for 25 minutes. Makes 24

13. Cauliflower cups

- $1^1/_2$ cups cauliflower rice

- $1/_4$ cup diced onion

- $1/_2$ cup shredded pepper jack cheese

- $1/_2$ teaspoon dried oregano

- $1/_2$ teaspoon dried basil

- $1/_2$ teaspoon salt

- 1 large egg, lightly beaten

1 Preheat oven to 350°F.

2 Combine all ingredients in a large mixing bowl and stir to incorporate.

3 Scoop mixture into the wells of a mini muffin tin and pack lightly.

4 Bake 30 minutes or until cups start to crisp. Allow to cool slightly and remove from tin.

14. Mac and Cheese Cups

Ingredients

- 8 oz elbow macaroni
- 2 tbsp salted butter
- 1/4 tsp paprika (use smoked paprika if you have it)
- 2 tbsp flour
- 1/2 cup whole milk
- 8 oz sharp cheddar cheese grated
- chopped chives or scallions for garnish
- butter for greasing the pan

Directions:

a) Grease a non-stick: mini muffin pan very well with butter or non-stick: cooking spray. Preheat the oven to 400 degrees F.

b) Bring a pot of salted water to a boil over high heat, then cook the pasta for 2 minutes less than the package says.

c) Melt the butter and add the paprika. Add the flour and stir the mixture around for 2 minutes. While whisking, add the milk.

d) Remove the pot from the heat and add the cheeses and drained pasta, stirring it all together until the cheese and sauce are well distributed.

e) Portion your mac and cheese into the muffin cups, either with a spoon or a 3-tbsp cookie scoop.

f) Bake the mac and cheese cups for 15 minutes, until bubbling and gooey.

15. Bologna quiche cups

Ingredient

- 12 Slices bologna

- 2 Eggs

- ½ cup   Biscuit mix

- ½ cup   Shredded sharp cheese

- ¼ cup   Sweet pickle relish

- 1 cup   Milk

a) Place bologna slices in lightly greased muffin tins to form cups.

b) Mix together remaining ingredients. Pour into bologna cups.

c) Bake at (400F) for 20-25 minutes or until golden.

16. Muffin prosciutto cup

- 1 slice prosciutto (about $1/2$ ounce)

- 1 medium egg yolk

- 3 tablespoons diced Brie

- 2 tablespoons diced mozzarella cheese

- 3 tablespoons grated Parmesan cheese

1 Preheat oven to 350°F. Take out a muffin tin with wells about $2^{1}/_{2}$" wide and $1^{1}/_{2}$" deep.

2 Fold prosciutto slice in half so it becomes almost square. Place it in muffin tin well to line it completely.

3 Place egg yolk into prosciutto cup.

4 Add cheeses on top of egg yolk gently without breaking it.

5 Bake about 12 minutes until yolk is cooked and warm but still runny.

6 Let cool 10 minutes before removing from muffin tin.

17. Brussel sprouts cups

Ingredient

- 12 mediums Brussels sprouts

- 6 ounces Yukon Gold potatoes

- 2 tablespoons Skim milk

- 1 tablespoon Olive oil

- $\frac{1}{8}$ teaspoon Salt

- 2 ounces Smoked trout, skinned

- 1 Roasted red pepper, cut into 2 inch by 1/8 inch strips

a) Preheat oven to 350

b) Trim stems, cut in half lengthwise, remove core leaving cups of darker green leaves.

c) Steam sprout cups for 6 minutes or until they're tender when pierced with a sharp knife and are still bright green.

d) Drain upside down on paper towels. Cook pototoes until tender , drain, adOd milk, olive oil and salt.

e) Beat until smooth. Gently fold in trout. $+\frac{1}{4}$> spoon into shells and place pepper strips on top.

18. Endive cups

- 1 large hard-boiled egg, peeled

- 2 tablespoons canned tuna in olive oil, drained

- 2 tablespoons avocado pulp

- 1 teaspoon fresh lime juice

- 1 tablespoon mayonnaise

- $^1/_8$ teaspoon sea salt

- $^1/_8$ teaspoon black pepper

- 4 Belgian endive leaves, washed and dried

1 In a small food processor, mix all ingredients except endive until well blended.

2 Scoop 1 tablespoon tuna mixture onto each endive cup.

3 Serve immediately.

19. Taco cups

- Chili powder,Cumin, paprika

- Salt, black pepper

- $1/4$ teaspoon dried oregano

- $1/4$ teaspoon crushed red pepper flakes

- $1/4$ teaspoon granulated garlic

- $1/4$ teaspoon granulated onion

- 1 pound 75% lean ground beef

- 8 (1-ounce) slices sharp Cheddar cheese

- $^{1}/_{2}$ cup no-sugar-added salsa

- $^{1}/_{4}$ cup chopped cilantro

- 3 tablespoons Frank's RedHot sauce

1 Preheat oven to 375°F. Line a baking sheet with parchment paper.

2 Combine spices in a small bowl and stir to mix. Cook ground beef in a medium skillet over medium-high heat. When beef is almost done cooking, add spice mixture and stir to coat completely. Remove from heat and set aside.

3 Arrange Cheddar cheese slices on lined baking sheet. Bake in preheated oven 5 minutes or until starting to brown. Allow to cool 3 minutes and then peel from baking sheet and transfer each slice to the well of a muffin tin, forming a cup. Allow to cool.

4 Scoop equal amounts of meat into each cup and top with 1 tablespoon of salsa. Sprinkle cilantro and hot sauce on top.

20. Ham 'n' cheddar cups

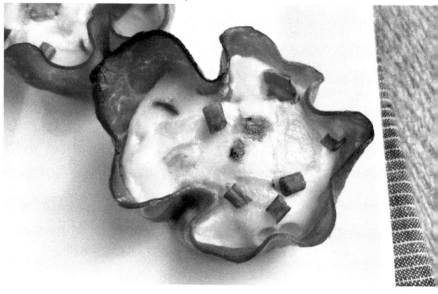

Ingredient

- 2 cups All-purpose flour

- ¼ cup Sugar

- 2 teaspoons Baking powder

- 1 teaspoon Salt

- ¼ teaspoon Pepper

- 6 Eggs

- 1 cup Milk

- $\frac{1}{2}$ pounds Fully cooked ham; cubed

- $\frac{1}{2}$ pounds Cheddar cheese; diced or shredded

- $\frac{1}{2}$ pounds Sliced bacon; cooked and crumbled

- 1 small Onion; finely chopped

a) In bowl, combine the flour, sugar, baking powder, salt and pepper. Beat eggs and milk; stir into dry ingredients until well mixed. Stir in ham, cheese, bacon and onion.

b) Fill well-greased muffin cups three-fourths full.

c) Bake at 350° for 45 minutes. Cool for 10 minutes before removing to a wire rack.

CRUDITES

21. Crudites with relish

Ingredient

- 2 teaspoons Olive oil

- 1 cup Finely chopped onion

- 1 tablespoon Chopped garlic

- 1 cup Canned crushed tomatoes

- 1 teaspoon Fresh lemon juice

- $\frac{1}{4}$ cup sun-dried tomatoes

- $\frac{1}{4}$ cup Pitted green olives; (about 10)

- ¼ cup (packed) fresh basil leaves

- 4 larges Drained canned artichoke hearts

- 2 tablespoons Chopped fresh parsley

- 2 tablespoons Toasted pine nuts

- Assorted vegetables

a) Heat oil in medium non-stick: skillet over medium heat. Add onion and sauté until just beginning to soften, about 3 minutes. Add garlic; sauté 30 seconds. Stir in canned tomatoes and lemon juice. Bring to simmer. Remove from heat.

b) Combine sun-dried tomatoes and next 5 ingredients in processor. Using on/off turns, process until vegetables are finely chopped. Transfer to medium bowl. Stir in tomato mixture. Season with salt and pepper.

22. Green and white crudites

Ingredient

- ½ cup Plain yogurt

- ½ cup Sour cream

- ½ cup Mayonnaise

- 1½ teaspoon White-wine vinegar; or to taste

- 1½ teaspoon Coarse-grained mustard

- 1 large Garlic clove; minced and mashed

- 1 teaspoon Aniseed; crushed

- 2 teaspoons Pernod; or to taste

- 1½ tablespoon Minced tarragon leaves

- 12 cups Assorted crudités

a) In a bowl whisk together all ingredients except herbs with salt and pepper to taste. Chill dip, covered, at least 4 hours and up to 4 days. Just before serving, stir in tarragon and chervil.

b) Arrange crudités decoratively on a tiered serving plate or in a large basket and serve with dip.

23. Kohlrabi crudites

Ingredient

- ½ cup Soy sauce; light

- ½ cup Rice vinegar

- 1 teaspoon Sesame seeds; toasted

- 1 tablespoon Scallions; minced

- 4 cups Kohlrabi slices; cut into chunks

a) Combine soy sauce, vinegar, sesame seeds and scallions.

b) Serve in a bowl surrounded by Kohlrabi chunks. Provide picks for eating.

24. Remoulade with vegetable crudites

Ingredient

- ½ cup Creole or brown mustard

- ½ cup Salad oil

- ¼ cup Catsup

- ¼ cup Cider vinegar

- ¼ teaspoon Tabasco sauce

- 2 tablespoons Finely chopped celery

- 2 tablespoons Finely chopped onion

- 2 tablespoons Finely chopped green pepper

- Cherry tomatoes

- Mushroom slices

- Cucumber slices

- Celery slices

- Carrot slices

a) Combine mustard, oil, catsup, vinegar, Tabasco and chopped vegetables; cover and chill.

b) Serve dip with whole and sliced vegetables.

25. Skeleton crudite

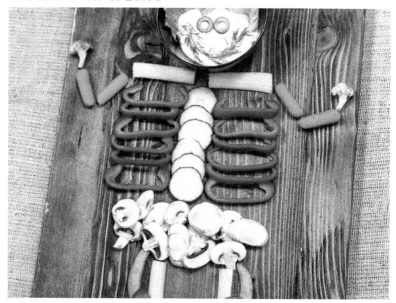

Ingredient

- 3 cups Low fat yogurt

- 1 cup Mayo

- ½ cup Peach jam

- 1 teaspoon orange juice

- ½ teaspoon Curry powder

- ½ teaspoon Pepper.

Skeleton Ingredients

- 1 zucchini sliced in half lengthwise

- 1 yellow squash sliced in half
- 6 ribs celery cut in half lengthwise
- 1 cucumber sliced into wedges
- 1 carrot cut into sticks
- 10 baby carrot fingers
- 1 red pepper cut into2 inch thick strips
- 1 yellow pepper cut into 2 inch thick strips
- 2 brocolli florets/ 2 cauliflower florets
- 10 snow peas /2 cherry tomatoes
- 2 mushrooms/1 radish
- 4 green beans /2 yellow beans

a) Stir together 3 cups low fat yogurt, 1 cup mayo, $\frac{1}{2}$ cup peach jam, 1 tsb orange juice, $\frac{1}{2}$ tsp curry powder and $\frac{1}{2}$ tsp pepper in a skull size bowl or scooped-out head of lettuce. Refrigerate.

b) Assemble skeleton

26. Spicy winter crudite

Ingredient

- 1 Red onion; peeled sliced

- 1 Green pepper; seeded and cut

- 1 Red or yellow pepper; seeded and cut

- 1 Turnip; peeled and thinly

- 2 cups Cauliflower florets

- 2 cups Broccoli florets

- 1 cup Baby carrots; trimmed

- $\frac{1}{2}$ cup Thinly sliced radishes

- 2 tablespoons Salt

- 1½ cup Olive oil

- 1 Yellow onion; peeled and finely; chopped

- ⅛ teaspoon Saffron threads

- Pinch Turmeric,Ground cumin,black pepper,Paprika,Cayenne, Salt

a) Place the prepared vegetables in a large bowl, sprinkle them with the 2 tablespoons of salt, and add the cold water.

b) The next day, drain and rinse the vegetables. Prepare the marinade by simmering the onion, spices, and salt in the olive oil for 10 minutes.

c) Spread the vegetables in a 9 x 13 inch dish. Pour the hot marinade over them.

d) Transfer to a decorative bowl to serve, either cold or at room temperature.

27. Tricolor crudites platter

Ingredient

- ¼ cup Plus 1T red wine vinegar

- 3 tablespoons Dijon mustard

- ½ cup Plus 2 T olive oil

- 2 tablespoons Minced fresh basil OR

- 2 teaspoons Dried basil

- 2 tablespoons Minced fresh chives or

- Green onions

- 1 teaspoon Minced fresh rosemary
- 2 Large cucumbers, peeled,
- 2 teaspoons Salt
- 2 Large raw beets, peeled, grated
- 2 Large carrots, peeled, grated
- 2 Large zucchini, grated
- 1 Bunch radishes, trimmed

a) Whisk vinegar and Dijon mustard to blend in small bowl. Gradually whisk in olive oil. Mix in basil, chives and rosemary. Season with salt and pepper.

b) Toss cucumbers and 2 teaspoons salt in bowl. Let stand 1 hour. Rinse and drain well. Place cucumbers in small bowl; add enough dressing to coat.

c) Place beets, carrots and zucchini in separate bowls. Toss each vegetable with enough dressing to coat.

28. Mound vegetables on platter

Ingredient

- 1 cup Canned corn, drained

- 1 small Green onion, chopped

- 1 Green pepper, chopped

- 1 Garlic clove, minced

- 1 largevFresh tomato, chopped

- $\frac{1}{4}$ cup Fresh parsley, chopped

- $\frac{1}{4}$ cup Extra virgin olive oil

- 2 tablespoons Balsamic vinegar

- Salt, Pepper

- 1 Scallion, chopped

a) Mix corn with onion, green pepper, garlic and tomato. In a separate small bowl or cup, mix olive oil and vinegar.

b) Pour over vegetable, toss with parsley; season with salt and pepper. Garnish each serving with scallions.

PARTY DIPS

29. Crab rangoon dip

- 1 (8-ounce) package cream cheese, softened to room temperature

- 2 tablespoons olive oil mayonnaise

- 1 tablespoon freshly squeezed lemon juice

- $1/2$ teaspoon sea salt

- $1/4$ teaspoon black pepper

- 2 cloves garlic, minced

- 2 medium green onions, diced

- $1/2$ cup shredded Parmesan cheese

- 4 ounces (about $1/2$ cup) canned white crabmeat

a) Preheat oven to 350°F.

b) In a medium bowl, mix cream cheese, mayonnaise, lemon juice, salt, and pepper with a hand blender until well incorporated.

c) Add garlic, onions, Parmesan cheese, and crabmeat and fold into mixture with a spatula.

d) Transfer mixture to an oven-safe crock and spread out evenly.

e) Bake 30–35 minutes until top of dip is slightly browned. Serve warm.

30. Goat Cheese Guacamole

Serves: 4-6

Ingredients

- 2 avocados
- 3 ounces goat cheese
- zest from 2 limes
- lemon juice from 2 limes
- $\frac{3}{4}$ teaspoon garlic powder
- $\frac{3}{4}$ teaspoon onion powder
- $\frac{1}{2}$ teaspoon salt
- $\frac{1}{4}$ teaspoon red pepper flakes (optional)
- $\frac{1}{4}$ teaspoon pepper

Directions:

a) Add avocados to a food processor and blend until smooth. Add rest of ingredients and blend until incorporated.

b) Serve with chips.

31. Bavarian party dip/spread

Yield: 1 1/4 pound

Ingredient

- $\frac{1}{2}$ cup   Onions, minced

- 1 pounds Kahn's Bavarian Brand Braunschweiger

- 3 ounces Cream cheese

- $\frac{1}{4}$ teaspoon   Black pepper

a) Sauté the onions 8-10 minutes, stirring frequently; remove from heat and drain. Remove the casing from Kahn's Bavarian Brand Braunschweiger and mix meat with the cream cheese until smooth. Mix in onions and pepper.

b) Serve as a liver spread on crackers, thinly sliced party rye or serve as a dip accompanied by a variety of fresh raw vegetables like carrots, celery, broccoli, radishes, cauliflower or cherry tomatoes.

32. Baked artichoke party dip

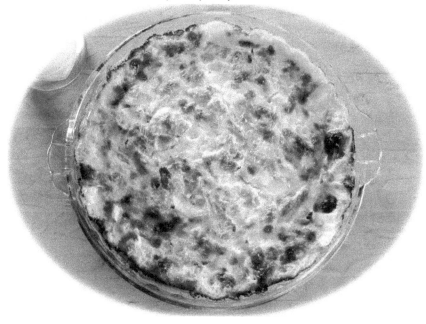

Ingredient

- 1 Loaf large dark rye bread

- 2 tablespoons   Butter

- 1 bunch   Green onions; chopped

- 6 Cloves of fresh garlic; minced finely, up to 8

- 8 ounces Cream cheese; at room temp.

- 16 ounces Sour cream

- 12 ounces Shredded cheddar cheese

- 1 can (14 oz.) artichoke hearts; drained and cut into quarters (water packed not marinated)

a) Cut a hole in the top of the bread loaf about 5 inches in diameter. Remove soft bread from cut portion and discard. Reserve crust to make top for loaf.

b) Scoop out most of the soft inside portion of the loaf and save for other purposes, such as stuffing or dried bread crumbs. In the butter,

c) Sauté the green onions and the garlic until the onions wilt. Cut the cream cheese into small chunks, add the onions, garlic, sour cream and cheddar cheese. Mix well. Fold in artichoke hearts, Out all of this mixture into hollowed out bread. Place top on bread and wrap in a couble thickness of heavy duty aluminium foil. Bake in 350 degree oven for $1\frac{1}{2}$ hours.

d) When ready, remove foil and serve, using cocktail rye bread to dip out the sauce.

33. Buffalo chicken dip

- 1 (8-ounce) package cream cheese

- $^1/_2$ cup Frank's Red-Hot sauce

- $^1/_4$ cup full-fat canned coconut milk

- $1^1/_2$ cups shredded cooked chicken

- $^3/_4$ cup shredded mozzarella cheese, divided

- $^1/_2$ cup blue cheese crumbles

1 Add cream cheese to a medium saucepan and heat over medium-low heat until melted. Stir in hot sauce and coconut milk.

2 When combined, add chicken until heated through.

3 Remove from heat and stir in $1/2$ cup mozzarella cheese and blue cheese crumbles.

4 Transfer to an 8" × 8" baking dish and sprinkle remaining mozzarella cheese on top. Bake 15 minutes or until cheese is bubbly. Serve warm.

34. Pizza dip

- 1 (8-ounce) package cream cheese, softened

- $1/2$ cup plain Greek yogurt

- 1 teaspoon dried oregano

- $1/4$ teaspoon dried basil

- $1/2$ teaspoon granulated onion

- $1/2$ teaspoon granulated garlic

- $3/4$ cup no-sugar-added pizza sauce

- $1/2$ cup shredded mozzarella cheese

- $1/4$ teaspoon salt

- $1/4$ teaspoon black pepper

1 Preheat oven to 350°F.

2 Combine cream cheese, yogurt, oregano, basil, onion, and garlic in a medium bowl and mix with a hand-held mixer until combined. Spread mixture into the bottom of an 8" × 8" baking pan.

3 Spread pizza sauce on top of cream cheese mixture, sprinkle with mozzarella cheese, and top with salt and pepper.

4 Bake covered 15 minutes. Remove cover and bake an additional 10 minutes or until cheese is golden and bubbly.

35. Ranch dip

- 1 cup mayonnaise

- $^{1}/_{2}$ cup plain Greek yogurt

- $1^{1}/_{2}$ teaspoons dried chives

- $1^{1}/_{2}$ teaspoons dried parsley

- $1^{1}/_{2}$ teaspoons dried dill

- $^{3}/_{4}$ teaspoon granulated garlic

- $^{3}/_{4}$ teaspoon granulated onion

- $^1/_2$ teaspoon salt

- $^1/_4$ teaspoon black pepper

1 Combine all ingredients in a small bowl.

2 Allow to sit in the refrigerator 30 minutes before serving.

36. Spicy shrimp and cheese dip

- 2 slices no-sugar-added bacon

- 2 medium yellow onions, peeled and diced

- 2 cloves garlic, minced

- 1 cup popcorn shrimp (not the breaded kind), cooked

- 1 medium tomato, diced

- 3 cups shredded Monterey jack cheese

- $1/4$ teaspoon Frank's RedHot sauce

- ¹/₄ teaspoon cayenne pepper

- ¹/₄ teaspoon black pepper

1 Cook the bacon in a medium skillet over medium heat until crisp, about 5–10 minutes. Keep grease in pan. Lay the bacon on a paper towel to cool. When cool, crumble the bacon with your fingers.

2 Add the onion and garlic to the bacon drippings in the skillet and sauté over medium-low heat until they are soft and fragrant, about 10 minutes.

3 Combine all the ingredients in a slow cooker; stir well. Cook covered on low setting 1–2 hours or until cheese is fully melted.

37. Garlic and bacon dip

- 8 slices no-sugar-added bacon

- 2 cups chopped spinach

- 1 (8-ounce) package cream cheese, softened

- $1/4$ cup full-fat sour cream

- $1/4$ cup plain full-fat Greek yogurt

- 2 tablespoons chopped fresh parsley

- 1 tablespoon lemon juice

- 6 cloves roasted garlic, mashed

- 1 teaspoon salt

- $1/2$ teaspoon black pepper

- $1/2$ cup grated Parmesan cheese

1 Preheat oven to 350°F.

2 Cook bacon in a medium skillet over medium heat until crispy. Remove bacon from pan and set aside on a plate lined with paper towels.

3 Add spinach to hot pan and cook until wilted. Remove from heat and set aside.

4 To a medium bowl, add cream cheese, sour cream, yogurt, parsley, lemon juice, garlic, salt, and pepper and beat with a hand-held mixer until combined.

5 Roughly chop bacon and stir into cream cheese mixture. Stir in spinach and Parmesan cheese.

6 Transfer to an 8" × 8" baking pan and bake 30 minutes or until hot and bubbly.

38. Creamy Goat Cheese Pesto Dip

INGREDIENTS

- 2 cups packed fresh basil leaves
- $\frac{1}{2}$ cup grated parmesan cheese
- 8 ounces goat cheese
- 1 -2 teaspoons minced garlic
- $\frac{1}{2}$ teaspoon salt
- $\frac{1}{2}$ cup olive oil

Directions:

a) Mix basil, cheeses, garlic and salt in a food processor or blender until smooth. Add olive oil in even stream and mix until combined.

b) Serve immediately or store in refrigerator.

39. Hot Pizza Super dip

Ingredients:

- Softened Cream Cheese
- Mayonnaise
- Mozzarella Cheese
- Basil
- Oregano
- Garlic Powder
- Pepperoni
- Black Olives
- Green Bell Peppers

Directions::

a) Mix in your softened cream cheese, mayonnaise and a little bit of mozzarella cheese. Add a sprinkle of basil, oregano, parsley and garlic powder, stir until its nicely combined.

b) Fill it in to your deep dish pie plate and spread it out in an even layer.

c) Spread your pizza sauce on top and add your preferred toppings. For this example, we will add mozzarella cheese, pepperoni black olives and green peppers. Bake at 350 for 20 minutes.

40. Baked Spinach and Artichoke Dip

Ingredients

- 14 oz can un-marinated artichoke hearts, drained and coarsely chopped
- 10 oz frozen chopped spinach thawed
- 1 cup HELLMANN'S real mayo p.s. the original recipe calls for Light mayo to cut calories
- 1 cup grated parmesan cheese
- 1 garlic clove pressed

Directions:

a) Thaw frozen spinach then squeeze it dry with your hands.

b) Stir together: drained & chopped artichoke, squeezed spinach, 1 cup mayo, 3/4 cup parmesan cheese, 1 pressed garlic clove and transfer to a 1-quart casserole or pie dish. Sprinkle on remaining 1/4 cup parmesan cheese.

c) Bake uncovered for 25 minutes at 350°F or until heated through. Serve with your favorite crostini, chips, or crackers.

PARTY POPS

41. Bacon And Goat Cheese Pops

INGREDIENTS

- 8 slices of bacon, cooked until crispy
- 4 ounces of goat cheese
- 4 ounces of cream cheese (not whipped!)
- 1 teaspoon honey
- 1 teaspoon thyme
- 2 tablespoons parsley, finely chopped
- 1/2 teaspoon freshly cracked pepper
- 20 baked apple chips (you will need to use 2 apples)

Directions:

a) Pat each piece of cooked bacon with paper towel to remove any grease. Finely chop the bacon and place in a small bowl. Add the thyme, parsley, and fresh cracked pepper and toss to combine. Set aside.

b) In a medium bowl add the goat cheese, cream cheese, and honey. Using a fork or wooden spoon mix until well combined.

c) Roll goat cheese mixture into thumb-sized balls. Roll each of these balls in the bacon mixture. Set aside on a baking sheet. Store balls, covered with a piece of saran wrap, in your fridge until ready to serve.

d) Place 1 goat cheese ball on top of each baked apple chip. Insert a lollipop stick into the top of each goat cheese ball

42. Coconut vanilla popsicles

- 2 cups unsweetened coconut cream, chilled

- $1/4$ cup unsweetened shredded coconut

- 1 teaspoon vanilla extract

- $1/4$ cup erythritol or granular Swerve

1 Place all ingredients in a blender and blend until completely mixed, about 30 seconds.

2 Pour mix into 8 popsicle molds, tapping molds to dislodge air bubbles.

3 Freeze at least 8 hours or overnight.

4 Remove popsicles from molds. If popsicles are hard to remove, run molds under hot water briefly, and popsicles will come loose.

43. Frozen fudge popsicles

Ingredient
- 1 pack   (3 3/4 oz) Chocolate Fudge
- Pudding & pie filling.
- 2 tablespoons   Sugar
- 3 cups   Milk

a) Combine the pudding mix, sugar and milk in a saucepan. Cook over medium heat, stirring constantly, until the mixture comes to a full boil. Remove from the heat and cool 5 mins. stirring twice. Place in the freezer about 30 minutes to cool and thicken. Spoon the mixture into the 10 three oz paper cups and insert a wooden popsicle stick or plastic spoon into each cup. Cover each cup with foil after cutting a small hole just large enough to poke stick or spoon handle through.

b) The foil helps to position the sticks upright and will keep the popsicles from dehydrating. Freeze until firm. Cut away the paper cups before serving

44. Orange Cranberry popsicles

Ingredient

- 1 (6 oz) can frozen orange juice concentrate, softened
- Or wuse grape juice, cranberry juice
- 1 (6 oz) can water
- 1 pint   Vanilla ice cream, softened, or 2 containers of
- Plain yogurt
- Popsicle sticks

- Cups

a) Whir in a blender. Pour into molds, insert sticks, and freeze.

45. Polynesian popsicles

- 1 cup skim milk
- 1 envelope unflavored gelatin
- $\frac{1}{2}$ cup honey or sugar
- 1 egg white
- $1\frac{1}{4}$ cups apricot nectar or canned pineapple juice
- popsicle sticks and cups

a) Pour milk into blender and add gelatin. Let soften for one minute before adding the rest of the ingredients to whip.
b) Pour into molds, insert sticks, and freeze.

46. Peach Whip Cream CREAMSICLES

- 1 (6 oz) can peaches in light syrup or 2 fresh ripe peaches, sliced and pitted
- 1 cup heavy cream
- 1 tsp sugar or honey (optional)
- popsicle sticks and cups

a) Whip cream in a blender for 30-45 seconds. Add peaches and honey.
b) Whir until smooth. Pour into molds, insert sticks, and freeze.

47. Chocolate pops

- 1 (8 oz) container plain yogurt
- 2 tbsp cocoa or carob powder
- 2 tbsp brown sugar or honey
- popsicle sticks and cups

a) Liquify in a blender, pour into molds, insert popsicle sticks, and freeze.

48. Glass snow cones

a) Freeze orange juice (or any other flavored juice) in ice cube trays, Pop frozen juice cubes in a plastic bag to store.

b) Put three to six of these cubes at a time in a blender.

c) Turn blender on and off until cubes reach snowy consistency. Pile into a cup to serve.

d) The whole batch blended at once will keep its carnival consistency stored in a container in the freezer. Kids can serve themselves.

e) Adding a little water makes it a "slush". Even kids who don't care for orange juice like it this way.

49. Watermelon popsicles

- 1 cup seedless watermelon chunks
- 1 cup orange juice
- 1 cup water popsicle
- sticks and cups

a) Blend these ingredients into a blender, pour into molds, insert sticks, and freeze.
b) Serve

50. Matcha popsicles

- 2 cups unsweetened coconut cream, chilled

- 2 tablespoons coconut oil

- 1 teaspoon matcha

- $1/4$ cup erythritol or granular Swerve

1 Place all ingredients in a blender and blend until completely mixed, about 30 seconds.

2 Pour mix into 8 popsicle molds, tapping molds to dislodge air bubbles.

3 Freeze at least 8 hours or overnight.

4 Remove popsicles from molds. If popsicles are hard to remove, run molds under hot water briefly, and popsicles will come loose.

CONCLUSION

Thank you for reaching this point.

The possibilities are endless. There are so many different types of finger food appetizers you can serve before dinner!

If you do not have the time or bandwidth to assemble 60 mini sliders, don't do it! If you can't afford crab claws, go with something that is inexpensive and budget-friendly!

If your guests are keto, GF, vegetarian, vegan or have other allergies, you may want to serve appetizers that safely check off all the boxes OR have a few different varieties for each guest to be happy with.

Lightning Source UK Ltd.
Milton Keynes UK
UKHW020645100621
385263UK00001B/145